HYDROPLANE RACING
IN THE TRI-CITIES

Four speeding hydroplanes are backlit as they thunder across the starting line for the final heat of the 2006 Columbia Cup in Tri-Cities. (Courtesy of Bill Osborne.)

FRONT COVER: Dave Villwock in the *Miss Budweiser*, Mark Weber in the *Diamond Lil's*, and Steve David in the *Oh Boy! Oberto* slide into the first turn of the 2001 Columbia Cup. (Courtesy of F. Pierce Williams.)

COVER BACKGROUND: For over 40 years, tens of thousands of fans have been coming to the banks of the Columbia River to bask in the sun and watch the world's fastest boats race for the Columbia Cup. (Courtesy of Clark Denslow.)

BACK COVER: Author David Williams gets a wild ride from the U-48 *Lakeridge Paving* at the 2007 Columbia Cup. (Courtesy of Chris Denslow.)

HYDROPLANE RACING
IN THE TRI-CITIES

David D. Williams

ARCADIA
PUBLISHING

Published by Arcadia Publishing
Charleston SC, Chicago IL, Portsmouth NH, San Francisco CA

Library of Congress Catalog Card Number: 2007941845

For all general information contact Arcadia Publishing at:
Telephone 843-853-2070
Fax 843-853-0044
E-mail sales@arcadiapublishing.com
For customer service and orders:
Toll-Free 1-888-313-2665

Visit us on the Internet at www.arcadiapublishing.com

CONTENTS

ACKNOWLEDGMENTS

The Tri-Cities Unlimited race has been a community effort for over 40 years, but there is one person whose efforts stand out beyond all others. Ken Maurer has been deeply involved with the race from the very beginning, and he has guided it through good times and bad. He, more than any other individual, is responsible for the Water Follies position as one of the longest running and most successful community festivals in the nation! For that reason, I am very proud to dedicate this book to Ken Maurer.

—David D. Williams

Visit the Hydroplane and Raceboat Museum at
5917 S 196th Street
Kent, WA 98032
Or log on to: www.thunderboats.org

The incomparable Bill Osborne took many of the photographs in this book. His talent for catching the beauty, power, and grace of unlimited racing is unmatched. To see more of his work, log on to www.billophoto.com.

Photographs not provided by Bill Osborne come from the extraordinary photograph collection of the Hydroplane and Raceboat Museum. Over the last 20 years, tens of thousands of photographs have been donated to the museum. Some were clearly marked by the original photographer; many were not. In preparing this book, I have attempted to identify and give proper credit to every photographer. I am continuing to research the origin of any unidentified photographer, and where possible, the photographer will be credited in future editions of this work.

INTRODUCTION

On July 4, 1803, Pres. Thomas Jefferson announced the purchase of 530 million square miles of real estate from France for an astounding $15 million. A few days later, Congress appropriated $2,500 to fund an expedition to explore the new territory and map a path to the West Coast. The expedition was lead by Meriwether Lewis and William Clark and included a 16-year-old Shoshone Indian woman named Sacagawea.

On October 16, 1805, the Lewis and Clark expedition stopped and spent a few nights at the confluence of the Snake and Columbia Rivers at a spot the local Native Americans called Great Forks. Forty-five years later, a gold prospector named John Commingers Ainsworth arrived at Great Forks and set up a ferry across the river. In 1875, when the Northern Pacific Railroad needed to build a bridge across the river, they too came to Great Forks, and Ainsworth's ferry crossing was incorporated into the town of Ainsworth. The small town was victim to frequent flooding, and when the bridge was completed in 1886, the town was moved a couple of miles northwest to higher ground. One of the Northern Pacific engineers involved in moving the town was named Virgil Bouge. Bouge had just returned from a construction project in the Peruvian Andes where he worked building the railroad in Cerro de Pasco. While Bouge was in Cerro de Pasco he witnessed several vicious dust storms. There is no proof, but there is speculation that the frequent dust storms in Eastern Washington inspired Bouge to change Ainsworth's name to Pasco. Pasco was incorporated in 1891. In 1904, the small town of Kennewick was incorporated across the river from Pasco. The name Kennewick comes from the word Kin-i-wak from the language of the Chemnapum, Native Americans who were the region's first inhabitants. The word Kin-i-wak is often translated as either "Grassy Place" or "Winter Haven."

About 10 miles upriver from Pasco and Kennewick, Nelson Rich founded the town of Richland, which was incorporated in 1910.

In 1931, the land in Pasco where Lewis and Clark camped was deeded to the State of Washington and turned into Sacagawea State Park.

In 1943, the U.S. Army Corps of Engineers selected the nearby town of Hanford to be the location of the super-secret "Site W," which manufactured plutonium for the Manhattan Project (the U.S. effort to build an atomic bomb during World War II).

Plutonium from Hanford was used in the first successful atomic detonation at the Trinity site in New Mexico, as well as in the "Fat Man" bomb that was dropped on the Japanese city of Nagasaki.

The sudden influx of government employees and money brought to the region by the Hanford site spurred astronomical growth in the small towns of Pasco, Kennewick, and Richland. For example, between 1943 and 1945, the population of Richland grew from 240 people to 25,000. After the war, the region continued to grow as the cold war arms race fueled demand for more plutonium.

In 1948, the Pasco Lions Club decided to hold the first Pasco Water Follies to promote water sports in the area. Along with parades, water skiing, and sailing, the Water Follies featured limited inboard and outboard hydroplane races. The pits were located at Sacagawea State Park, and raceboats were hauled in and out of the water close to the location of the original Lewis and Clark campsite.

The Pasco Water Follies were a huge success and by 1965 had expanded to include Kennewick and Richland. The festival's name was changed to the Tri-Cities Water Follies. In 1966, the festival included unlimited hydroplanes for the first time, and since then, the Tri-Cities race has become a major stop on the unlimited circuit.

This book is the story of the Tri-Cities unlimited race and how it grew from a small local festival to a major national event.

Outboard racers take part in one of the first Pasco Water Follies events held at Sacagawea State Park in 1948. (Courtesy of the Tri-Cities Water Follies.)

1

1966–1972

THE EARLY YEARS

The Tri-Cities' love affair with unlimited hydroplane racing began in 1957, when a group of Tri-Cities businessmen led by Stan Adams bought Edgar Kaiser's *Scooter Too* and changed her name to *Tri-Tomic*. The black and white boat sported three electrons orbiting a nucleus on her tailfin. Before she ever raced, she went through another name change and was called *Adios* when she appeared at the Mile High Gold Cup on Lake Tahoe.

At that first race, *Adios* qualified with future *Miss Budweiser* crew chief George McKernan at the wheel but failed to finish a heat. In 1958, the boat was sold to George Gilham, and the team went to the Diamond Cup in Idaho, where they finished eighth out of 11 boats. In 1959, Gilham renamed the boat *Miss Tri-Cities* and took her to the Gold Cup race in Seattle but failed to qualify.

In 1965, an informal group of Water Follies board members enjoyed getting together in the bar at the Sahara Hotel in Pasco, knocking back a few beers, and talking about boat racing. One day, Jack Hamann, Mark Pence, Keith Bowers, Ken Maurer, and Wally Reid decided to hop into Jack's Cadillac and drive down to Lake Tahoe to watch the 1965 World Championship Race and learn how to host a race. The five friends took turns driving and paid for the expenses out of their own pockets. To show the rest of the racing community that they were serious, they gave Seattle's Bob Gilliam $1,500 to sponsor the U-88 for three races and called her the *Tri-City Sun*. The boat failed to qualify for the Seattle Gold Cup and the Lake Tahoe World Championship; she finally made it into a race in San Diego and finished 13th.

On November 17, 1965, the American Power Boat Association (APBA) awarded the Tri-Cities Water Follies a sanction to hold its first unlimited hydroplane race on July 24. The race would be called the Atomic Cup, and the course would be in a wide spot of the Columbia River behind McNary Dam called Lake Wallula, just north of the Highway 395 Bridge (known locally as the Blue Bridge). The pits would be in Columbia Park, and the prize money was $25,000!

Race chairman Jack Hamann led a team of hardworking Water Follies volunteers to get everything ready for the event. It was a huge task arranging for pit space, cranes, bleachers, parking, restrooms, concessions, security, and a thousand other details for a first-time race.

Unfortunately, the 1966 race was almost over before it started. Three devastating accidents (one just three weeks before the race) killed four of the nation's top drivers and destroyed four of the fastest boats. There was talk among fans that the season should be canceled, but the owners and drivers never wavered in their commitment to keep racing. Twelve teams showed up for the Atomic Cup, including Bob Gilliam and his aging U-37 *Miss Tri-Cities*, sponsored by the Tri-Cities Nuclear Council.

The fastest qualifier was Bill Cantrell and the *Smirnoff*, at 111.386 miles per hour. The weather was warm, sunny, and windy. Over 60,000 people paid $2 each to watch Bill Brow drive Bernie Little's *Miss Budweiser* to its first victory ever. It was a tough race, with both the *Miss Chrysler Crew* and *Tahoe Miss* leading the final heat before breaking down. The *Tri-City Herald* pronounced the race a "success—financially, artistically and safety wise." Owners and drivers agreed and promised to come back the following year.

In 1967, fifteen boats showed up for the Atomic Cup. Jim McCormick and the *Wayfarers Club Lady* were the top qualifiers at 110.837 miles per hour, but Bill Sterett in the *Chrysler Crew* was just a tick of the clock behind at 110.565, and Bill Muncey in the *Miss U.S.* was third at 110.294. Billy Schumacher won the race with a perfect day, winning all three heats in his new *Miss Bardahl*.

One of the fastest boats on the unlimited circuit in 1968 was Dave Heerensperger's *Miss Eagle Electric*, driven by Col. Warner Gardner. The "Screaming Eagle" was based out of Spokane, in eastern Washington, and Tri-City fans embraced the team as a hometown favorite. Colonel Gardner and the *Eagle* did not disappoint their supporters. They qualified fastest and won all three heats to claim victory in the third Atomic Cup. Six weeks later, Gardner was killed when the *Eagle* crashed in the final heat of the Detroit Gold Cup.

An estimated 92,000 sun-baked spectators watched eight boats battle for the 1969 Atomic Cup, but the racing action was not the only thing that was on their minds. Many fans carried transistor radios, listening between heats to news bulletins issued from NASA about the Apollo 11 lunar mission. Shortly after Bill Muncey and the *Miss U.S.* claimed victory in heat 1B, and just before the start of heat 2A, Neil Armstrong and Buzz Aldrin piloted the lunar lander to a perfect landing in the Sea of Tranquility on the moon! There was an audible cheer from fans all along the racecourse. Later that day, Dean Chenoweth drove the *Myr's Special* to a final-heat victory to claim the fourth annual Atomic Cup.

Tommy "Tucker" Fults drove Dave Heerensperger's *Lil' Buzzard* to victory in the 1970 race and, as in 1968, fans treated Heerensperger's victory like a home team victory. Unfortunately, just like in 1968, the victory was followed by tragedy when Fults was killed two months later when the *Lil' Buzzard* crashed while practicing for the Gold Cup in San Diego.

On July 4, 1971, the *Miss Madison*, an old and under-funded boat, shocked the world of unlimited racing by winning the Gold Cup in Madison. Many students of the sport thought that it was a fluke. The Madison team proved all doubters wrong when they backed up their Gold Cup with a win in the 1971 Atomic Cup.

In 1962, Bill Muncey claimed the national championship with the *Miss Thriftway* by winning every race on the circuit but one. In 1972, Muncey stormed back into the national championship for the first time in 10 years by winning every race on the circuit but one, including the seventh annual Atomic Cup.

The Adios crew poses in front of the boat with Pasco Waters Follies Beauty Queens in 1957. The *Adios* used a unique 24-cylinder "W"-configuration Allison engine that had 3,420 cubic inches of displacement and put out an estimated 4,000 horsepower! (Courtesy of the Tri-Cities Water Follies.)

George McKernan drove the first unlimited hydroplane to represent the Tri-Cities. He never won any races in the *Adios*, but years later, McKernan would become crew chief of the *Miss Budweiser*. As a crew chief, he won the very first Atomic Cup.

In 1965, the Tri-Cities Water Follies sponsored Bob Gilliam's U-88 for three races. The *Tri-City Sun* failed to qualify for the Gold Cup in Seattle and the World Championship race on Lake Tahoe and took 13th place at the San Diego Cup in San Diego. (Courtesy of the Tri-Cities Water Follies.)

In 1966, Bob Gilliam again ran a boat named *Tri-Cities*. This time his U-37 was sponsored by the Tri-Cities Nuclear Council and called *Miss Tri-Cities*. The U-37 was the former *Slo-mo-shun V*, which had won the Gold Cup in 1951 and 1954. The *Miss Tri-Cities* made it to four races and collected one 10th-place trophy and three 11th-place finishes.

Jack Hamann was a former outboard racer who began his racing career running boats from Sacagawea State Park during the early Pasco Water Follies. He was race chairman for the first unlimited race in 1966 and was responsible for pulling all of the various elements of the race together.

Keith Bowers was one of the five original board members who made the trip to Lake Tahoe in 1965 to research unlimited racing. He was pit chairman for the 1966 race and continued as a volunteer for many years, serving as board president in 1979.

The *Smirnoff*, with Bill Cantrell driving, was the first boat on the water when the course opened for qualifying for the 1966 race. She was also the fastest qualifier for the race. This boat was the second *Smirnoff*. The first boat had been destroyed in a horrible accident that killed veteran driver Chuck Thompson just three weeks before the Atomic Cup.

Washington State's strict blue laws, which prohibited advertising liquor on Sundays, presented a problem for the *Smirnoff*. The vodka bottle that appeared on the boat's tailfin was fine for Friday and Saturday test runs, but on Sunday, the bottle had to be covered. Luckily, Smirnoff's parent company, Heublein, produced other products that could be easily substituted.

The entire Tri-Cities community got wrapped up in "hydro fever." Here Sharon Haln shows off her "Atomic Roostertail" hairdo. (Courtesy of the Tri-Cities Water Follies.)

With more then 60,000 people showing up for the first race, traffic was bumper-to-bumper trying to get into Columbia Park. Parking was also difficult, with many fans having to walk more than a mile to get to the race. The 60,000-person attendance figure is astounding considering that the combined population of the Tri-Cities was less than 90,000 at the time. (Courtesy of the Tri-Cities Water Follies.)

Bill Brow drove Bernie Little's *Miss Budweiser* to victory in the first ever Atomic Cup. The boat that Brow drove replaced the primary *Miss Budweiser*, which had been destroyed a month earlier in an accident in Washington, D.C. The accident also took the lives of Don Wilson and Rex Manchester. (Courtesy of Bill Osborne.)

Bill Brow and Bernie Little are seen here receiving their first-place Atomic Cup trophy from the Water Follies queen and her court. The trophy actually contained a small chip of radioactive Cobalt 60 so that the Atomic Cup trophy would react to a Geiger counter. Little also received $5,000 in prize money for winning the race. From left to right are Bernie Little, Patty Wallace, Cathy Brown, Cheryl McKinnis, and Bill Brow. (Courtesy of Bill Osborne.)

Bill Brow never got a chance to defend his Atomic Cup victory. He was killed when the *Miss Budweiser* crashed in Tampa, Florida, at the first race of the 1967 season. A new *Miss Budweiser*, driven by rookie Mike Thomas, took fifth place in the 1967 Atomic Cup. (Courtesy of E. K. Muller.)

The twin-automotive-powered *Miss Chrysler Crew*, owned and driven by Bill Sterett Sr., took second place in the 1967 race. (Courtesy of Bob Carver.)

Billy Schumacher and the brand new Ed Karelsen–designed *Miss Bardahl* made a clean sweep of the Atomic Cup. Winning every heat entered, they took home $5,000 in prize money for winning the 1967 race. (Courtesy of Bob Carver.)

Twenty-four-year-old Billy Schumacher quickly earned the nickname "Billy the Kid," but his skill on the racecourse proved that he was much more than a kid. In 1967, he won six out of eight races, including the Gold Cup and Atomic Cup, on his way to the national championship.

Ray Forsman of Oak Harbor, Washington, launched his new, radical twin-automotive-powered cabover hydroplane. *The Dutchman* was designed and built by Forsman and was powered by two Ford V-8s. Unfortunately, it was not able to qualify.

Rookie driver Ray Forsman prepares to take the U-28 *Dutchman* out for a qualification attempt.

The fatal accidents that plagued the sport in 1966 and 1967 led to new design innovations in 1968. Three boats sported "pickle fork" bows that were designed to reduce the risk of a boat nosing in. This photograph shows two of the pickle-fork boats—*Harrah's Club* and *Smirnoff*—preparing to leave the Tri-Cities pits for heat 2B of the 1968 Atomic Cup. (Courtesy of Rich Ormbrek.)

The 1967 Atomic Cup Champion *Miss Bardahl* sported a new paint scheme for 1968. The *Bardahl* won two preliminary heats but broke a connecting rod on the second lap of the final heat and did not finish. (Courtesy of Rich Ormbrek.)

Warner Gardner had a perfect weekend at the 1968 Atomic Cup. He was fastest qualifier and won all three heats to give owner Dave Heerensperger his first Atomic Cup victory.

Miss Eagle Electric was built in 1962 as the *$-Bill* but had a lackluster career until Dave Heerensperger bought her and turned her over to crew chief Jack Cochran and driver Warner Gardner. They won three races in 1968 and were in contention for the national championship until the boat crashed in Detroit, killing Gardner.

When fans showed up for the 1969 race, they saw that the boat responsible for introducing the Tri-Cities to unlimited racing, the original *Miss Tri-Cities*, had been placed atop a pedestal at the entrance to Columbia Park. (Courtesy of Bill Osborne.)

The unlimited hydros are beautiful and spectacular and have always attracted photographers. One of the best is Bill Osborne, whose work makes up the bulk of this book. In this photograph, Bill is shooting action at the 1969 Atomic Cup.

Claudia Cole, wife of Phil Cole, then executive secretary of the Unlimited Racing Commission, shows off the 1969 Atomic Cup trophy to the racers. From left to right are Leif Borgersen, Ron Kasper, Bob Gilliam, Norm Evans, Tommy Fults, Bill Muncey, Dean Chenoweth, Bill Sterett, Walt Kade, and Jim McCormick.

The pits are a busy and colorful place on race day. Here Mike Wolfbauer's U-10 *Savair's Mist* is lowered into the water before the 1969 race. (Courtesy of Rich Ormbrek.)

The oldest boat in the pits at the 1969 race was the fastest boat in the race! Bob Fendler's *Atlas Van Lines*, built in 1957 as the *Miss Rocket*, turned in the fastest competition lap of the day (110.294 miles per hour), with Jim McCormick driving. (Courtesy of Rich Ormbrek.)

The newest boat in the pits was the slowest boat in the race! The brand new 1969 *Pride of Pay N' Pak* outrigger, with Tommy Fults driving, had the slowest qualifying speed at 91.033, barely enough to beat the 90.0-miles-per-hour minimum required to make the race.

Dean Chenoweth drove Lee Schoneith's *Myr's Special* to victory in the 1969 Atomic Cup. (Courtesy of Rich Ormbrek.)

The 1970 Atomic Cup got off to a rocky start for the Budweiser team. The boat stuffed (nosed in) during heat 1C and was badly damaged. Driver Dean Chenoweth was not seriously injured, and the boat was repaired in time to win the Seafair race in Seattle two weeks later. (Courtesy of Rich Ormbrek.)

Tommy Fults was one of the rising stars on the unlimited circuit in 1970. His movie-star good looks, flashing smile, and hard-charging tactics on the racecourse made him extremely popular with the fans. At the 1970 Atomic Cup, he qualified the *Lil Buzzard* at 107.656 miles per hour, tying Leif Borgersen and the *Notre Dame* for fastest qualifier.

Tommy Fults and the *Lil Buzzard* won the 1970 Atomic Cup, but two months later, while running for a low-speed photo shoot in San Diego, the *Buzzard* hit a wake left by Leif Borgersen and the *Notre Dame* and spun out, killing Fults. In an ironic twist of fate, Fults's widow, Suzie, ended up marrying Borgersen several years later. (Courtesy of Rich Ormbrek.)

In 1971, the *Miss Budweiser* was the two-time defending national champion and had one of the best drivers, highest-paid crew, and biggest sponsorship budgets, but they had rotten luck in Tri-Cities and were only able to finish one heat, settling for sixth place overall. (Courtesy of Bill Osborne.)

The *Pride of Pay N' Pak*, driven by Bill Schumacher, was the fastest qualifier at the 1971 Atomic Cup and won the first two heats. They only had to finish third place or better in the final to claim the victory, but a blown supercharger on the second lap caused the boat to go dead in the water. (Courtesy of Bill Osborne.)

Nineteen hundred seventy-one was a Cinderella year for the *Miss Madison* team. Their boat was 12 years old, they were using a lowly stock Allison compared to other teams' high-powered Merlins, and they had a small budget, but they managed to win the Gold Cup and the Atomic Cup. The success of the 1971 Madison team inspired the family-action movie *Madison*, released by MGM in 2005. (Courtesy of Bill Osborne.)

Bill Muncey dominated the sport of unlimited racing in the late 1950s and early 1960s, but a long dry spell caused many fans and sports writers to wonder if Bill's career was over. In fact, a *Seattle Times* reporter covering the 1971 Atomic Cup wrote a story asking, "Where's Bill Muncey?" The question was answered in 1972, when Muncey and the *Atlas Van Lines* won six out of seven races, including the Gold Cup, the Atomic Cup, and the national championship. (Courtesy of Bill Osborne.)

2

1973–1984

THE GOLD CUP YEARS

Since 1904, the premier trophy in powerboat racing has been the APBA Gold Cup. For decades, huge audiences, numbering in the hundreds of thousands, watched legends like Gar Wood, Guy Lombardo, and Bill Muncey fight for the cup.

One of the significant features of Gold Cup racing in the past was that the winning team got to host the next year's event on their home racecourse. That meant that the trophy would travel across the nation, and winning it was important to the local community. In 1962, that changed, and from 1963 on, the race went to the highest bidder. Bidding wars caused prize money to shoot up, and soon cities like Detroit, Seattle, and San Diego were offering prize packages that were double or even triple the amount of other race sites.

In 1971, the tiny town of Madison, Indiana, with a population of only 13,000, bid on the Gold Cup and hosted a very successful race, which incidentally was won by their hometown boat, *Miss Madison*.

Tiny Madison's success in staging the nation's foremost hydroplane race gave the Water Follies board confidence that they could do the same. Under the direction of Pres. Dave Dickerson and race chairman Ken Thompson, Tri-Cities successfully bid for the 1973 Gold Cup. Hosting such an important event was a huge job, but once more, the amazing Water Follies volunteers were up to the job.

Fifteen boats showed up for the race, but two boats—Bob Gilliam's *Valu Mart II* and Jim McCormick's *Redman Too*—failed to qualify.

Dave Heerensperger's brand new *Pay N' Pak* set a new two-and-a-half-mile course record, qualifying at 124.310 miles per hour and bettering the old record by almost eight miles an hour! The speedy new *Pay N' Pak*, with Mickey Remund driving, won all three of her preliminary heats and was well out in front in the final heat when she lost her propeller and began to sink. Dean Chenoweth and the *Miss Budweiser* easily passed the stricken *Pak* and went on to give owner Bernie Little his third Gold Cup.

In 1974, the Water Follies board skipped the Gold Cup and chose to put on the World Championship race. For the first time in many years, the World Championship really was an international affair, with the arrival of Stan Jones's *Solo* from Australia.

The *Pay N' Pak* was back, with George Henley replacing Mickey Remund in the cockpit. The "Winged Wonder," as fans now called the boat, qualified fastest and easily won the race. *Solo* failed to qualify.

The Gold Cup was back in 1975 and so was the *Pak*. George Henley pretty much had everything his way, as the *Pay N' Pak* won its three elimination heats and only had to coast home in third place to give Dave Heerensperger his second Gold Cup in a row. This would be the last Gold Cup to be awarded on points. Starting in 1976, the Gold Cup would feature a winner-take-all final heat.

In 1976, the Gold Cup went to Detroit, so the Water Follies unveiled their new Columbia Cup for the first time. Growing environmental concerns and antinuclear sentiment across the nation caused the Water Follies board to reconsider having their race named the Atomic Cup.

In the off-season between 1975 and 1976, Dave Heerensperger retired from the sport and sold his entire race team to Bill Muncey, who was sponsored by Atlas Van Lines. Muncey repainted the old *Pak* red, white, and blue to pay tribute to the nation's bicentennial and swept the field at Tri-Cities, tying the *Miss Budweiser* for fastest qualifier and winning the final heat after the *Bud* broke down.

The Gold Cup returned to the Columbia River in 1977, and Bill Muncey won the race with a breathtakingly perfect start in the final heat. While the other boats "trolled" up to the start at barely 100 miles per hour, Muncey hit the line at well over 170 and was far ahead before the rest of the fleet got to the first turn. It was Muncey's sixth Gold Cup victory and moved him ahead of the great Gar Wood for all-time Gold Cup wins.

The Columbia Cup returned to the Tri-Cities for six years, from 1978 to 1983. Ron Snyder and the *Miss Budweiser* won in 1978, and Bill Muncey and the *Atlas* scored back-to-back wins in 1979 and 1980. Chip Hanauer drove the *Squire Shop* to victory in 1981, Tom D'Eath won in 1982 driving a different *Squire Shop*, and Jack Schafer Jr. won the 1983 race in the *American Speedy Printing*.

The Gold Cup returned to the Tri-Cities one final time in 1984 with $85,000 dollars in prize money and a fleet of 16 boats. The 1984 race will long be remembered as a battle between the old, venerable piston engines and the new, high-tech turbine engines. The fastest qualifier was Bob Steil's Rolls Royce Merlin–powered *Squire Shop*, with Mickey Remund driving. Second on the qualifying ladder was Steve Woomers's turbine-powered *Miss Tosti Asti* with Steve Reynolds at the wheel. Third spot went to Bernie Little's Rolls Royce Griffon–powered *Miss Budweiser*, driven by Jim Kropfeld. Barely one mile an hour separated all three boats.

The final heat saw Mickey Remund get a flawless start and take a commanding lead into the first turn while the rest of the field staggered across the line late and out of position. The *Tosti* and *Bud* both fell out early, leaving only Chip Hanauer in the *Atlas Van Lines* to try and catch Remund in the *Squire Shop*. Remund and the old Merlin engine ran an amazing race, but the *Atlas* slowly gained. Finally, coming out of the west turn of the fifth lap, the *Squire's* motor belched a huge ball of flames, lost power, and sputtered to a halt. Chip and the *Atlas* swept around the outside and coasted to their third straight Gold Cup victory.

Ken Thompson, posing here with the Gold Cup in 1973, was the race chairman for the first Gold Cup in the Tri-Cities and one of the driving forces in making the race such a huge success. (Courtesy of the Tri-Cities Water Follies.)

Dean Chenoweth and the *Miss Budweiser* claimed $15,000 in prize money and the Gold Cup when they beat Dave Heerensperger's *Pay N' Pak* to win the 1973 Gold Cup. It was an especially hard loss for Heerensperger, because the boat that won the race was a former *Pay N' Pak* that he had sold to the Budweiser team. (Courtesy of Bill Osborne.)

The husband-and-wife team of Harry and Lucille Woods were an important part of the unlimited circuit. Harry was a referee and Lucille a scorer. They began working unlimited races in 1951. They are seen here posing with the 1974 World Championship trophy. (Courtesy of the Tri-Cities Water Follies.)

Australia's entry into the 1974 World Championship was the VS-41 *Solo*. Owned by Stan Jones, Bob Saniga, and Dick Carnie and driven by Saniga, she was a two-time Griffith Cup winner in Australia and had never lost a heat in her career. Two broken propellers while trying to qualify in Tri-Cities forced her to withdraw from the race. (Courtesy of Bill Osborne.)

The U-95, driven by Leif Borgersen, was the first turbine-powered unlimited to make it into a race. She was the second fastest qualifier for the race and beat the *Pay N' Pak* in heat 2C. She was damaged in a controversial accident in the final and finished a disappointing fourth. (Courtesy of Bill Osborne.)

The rules of unlimited racing limit the number of boats per heat to six. Sometimes an "alternate" seventh boat is allowed onto the course in case one of the other boats fails to start. If all six boats are running, though, the alternate must pull off. In the final heat of the 1974 Tri-Cities race, the alternate, Bill Muncey, failed to pull off, resulting in this famous "seven boat start." Muncey, in lane two, ended up colliding with the U-95 (barely visible outside of the rooster tail of the *Pay N' Pak* in lane four). This accident essentially ended the U-95's career. (Courtesy of Bill Osborne.)

The media quickly dubbed *Pay N' Pak's* new driver George Henley "Smiling George." His total, unabashed love for boat racing was always evident on his face. (Courtesy of Bill Osborne.)

The wing on the back of the *Pay N' Pak* inspired fans to refer to the boat as "The Winged Wonder." Henley and the *Pak* were an awesome combination in 1974, winning seven races, including the Tri-Cities World Championship, the Seattle Gold Cup, and the national championship. (Courtesy of Bill Osborne.)

Lee Schoenith had Jon Staduacher build him a new *Atlas Van Lines* for the 1975 season, but the boat never worked as well as hoped. She finished a disappointing eighth in the Tri-Cities Gold Cup and seventh overall in national high points. (Courtesy of Bill Osborne.)

The "Turbo Twins" (*Miss U.S.* and *Lincoln Thrift*) finished second and third in the Gold Cup. Both boats were built by Ron Jones and powered by turbocharged Allison engines. The *Miss U.S.* was driven by Tom D'Eath, and Milner Irvin drove the *Lincoln Thrift*. (Courtesy of Bill Osborne.)

This aerial shot of the run to the start of heat 1B shows a small portion of the huge crowd that attended the race. Shortly after this photograph was taken, the *Miss Budweiser* (second boat from the bottom) lost a large part of her left sponson and sank. (Courtesy of the Tri-Cities Water Follies.)

George Henley retired from racing after his stellar 1974 season. Jim McCormick took over the cockpit of the *Pay N' Pak*. After a lackluster performance in the first two races of the season, Dave Heerensperger coaxed Henley out of retirement. Henley and the *Pak* won the Gold Cup in Tri-Cities and went on to claim their second straight national championship. (Courtesy of Bill Osborne.)

The oldest boat in the pits for the 1976 Columbia Cup was the U-22 *Barney Armstrong's Machine*. Owned by Tad Dean, the boat was built in 1957 and was sponsored by the local rock group Barney Armstrong's Machine. (Courtesy of the Tri-Cities Water Follies)

The youngest driver in the pits for the 1976 Columbia Cup was 22-year-old Chip Hanauer (seen here being interviewed by *Seattle Post-Intelligencer* reporter Bill Knight), who was born in 1954, just three years before the *Barney Armstrong's Machine* that he would be driving was built. (Courtesy of Bill Osborne.)

Bill Schumacher drover Leslie Rosenberg's *Olympia Beer* to a second-place finish at the Columbia Cup in 1976. Schumacher won the drivers' championship in 1975 and finished second in 1976. (Courtesy of Bill Osborne.)

Mickey Remund and the *Miss Budweiser* grabbed the lead at the start of the final heat in the 1976 Columbia Cup. They looked to be sure winners, but the engine let go just before the start of the last lap. (Courtesy of Bill Osborne.)

Everyone knew that Bill Muncey was a great boat driver, but when he bought the Pay N' Pak team in 1976, there were serious questions about how well he could perform as an owner. He silenced all critics when he won five out of nine races, including the Columbia Cup and the national championship in his first year. (Courtesy of Bill Osborne.)

Few sights in the sporting world are as impressive as a field of unlimited hydroplanes running for the starting line. This exhibition run was staged on Saturday before the 1976 race. Photographs from this exhibition ended up on the front page of both the *Tri-City Herald* and the *Seattle Post-Intelligencer*. (Courtesy of Bill Osborne.)

Mickey Remund fires up the *Miss Budweiser* to attempt to qualify for the 1977 Gold Cup in Tri-Cities. The *Miss Budweiser* lost a propeller during Friday testing and tore up the bottom of the boat. The Bud crew took the damaged boat back to Don Kelson's shop in Seattle, made repairs, and returned to Tri-Cites in time to take second place in the race. (Courtesy of Bill Osborne.)

Bill Muncey brought the *Pay N' Pak* out of retirement for the 1977 Gold Cup. Ron Armstrong drove to victory in heat 1A, but the runner on the left sponson came off during heat 2C, and the *Pak* was done for the day. (Courtesy of Bill Osborne.)

Third place in the 1977 Gold Cup went to Jerry Bangs, driving Jerry Kalen's *Squire*. Bangs's promising career was cut short when he was thrown out the *Squire* and killed during an accident at the Seafair Race one week later. (Courtesy of Bill Osborne.)

Gar Wood won five Gold Cups between 1917 and 1921. It was a record that some thought would never be beaten. When Bill Muncey won his sixth Gold Cup in Tri-Cities in 1977, he celebrated by waving to the crowd during his victory lap. (Courtesy of Bill Osborne.)

By 1978, the former U-96 had gone through a couple of owners and was being raced by Chuck King with a Rolls Royce engine. She was called *Hawaiian Tropics* earlier in the season but was sponsored by Barney Armstrong's Machine in Tri-Cities. (Courtesy of Bill Osborne.)

Bob Maschmedt qualified Bill Wurster's *Oh Boy! Oberto* for the 1978 Columbia Cup but failed to finish a single heat due to mechanical woes. (Courtesy of Bill Osborne.)

Bill Muncey and the new cabover *Atlas Van Lines* won six out of seven races in 1978. Muncey was leading in the final heat in Tri-Cities when the engine let go, allowing Ron Snyder and the *Miss Budweiser* to claim the victory. (Courtesy of Bill Osborne.)

The Budweiser team celebrates their 1978 Columbia Cup Victory. From left to right are (first row) Lou Dersch, director of sales and promotion at Anheuser-Busch; Bernie Little, owner; Bill Penland; and Ray Runkle; (second row) Jack Gottwig, John Bianchi, Dave Culley, and driver Ron Snyder. (Courtesy of Bill Osborne.)

Steve Reynolds took top qualifying honors at the 1979 Columbia Cup in the *Miss Circus Circus* with a lap at 133.136 miles per hour. Unfortunately, the boat suffered significant damage when it lost its propeller on the second lap of heat 2A. (Courtesy of Bill Osborne.)

Longtime Water Follies board member Ken Thompson, who had served as race chairman from 1973 to 1978 and was board president in 1978, bought Bernie Little's eighth *Miss Budweiser* (the same boat that won the Columbia Cup in 1978) and campaigned it as *Miss Tri City Tile and Masonry*. In the 1979 race, the boat finished a disappointing eighth with veteran Jack Schafer at the wheel. (Courtesy of Bill Osborne.)

In 1979, Bernie Little introduced his new Rolls Royce Griffon–powered *Miss Budweiser*. The Griffon engine was about 600 cubic inches larger than the Rolls Royce Merlin and put out an estimated 1,000 extra horsepower. The new boat was driven by Dean Chenoweth and was very fast; however, teething pains kept her out of the winner's circle in 1979. (Courtesy of Bill Osborne.)

Once more, Bill Muncey and his "Blue Blaster" *Atlas Van Lines* proved unstoppable, winning every heat in the 1979 Columbia Cup. He won seven out of nine races that year, including the Gold Cup and the national championship. (Courtesy of Bill Osborne.)

During testing for the 1980 Columbia Cup, Bernie Little, an experienced airplane and helicopter pilot, took the mighty Griffon *Bud* out for a few test laps. Little often enjoyed taking his boats out for test spins, but this would be the last time that he drove. (Courtesy of Bill Osborne.)

The 1980 race saw the unveiling of Dave Heerensperger's new turbine-powered *Pay N' Pak*. The boat was designed and built by Jim Lucero, the winningest crew chief in the history of the sport. (Courtesy of Bill Osborne.)

The *Pay N' Pak* was very fast but was badly damaged in a spectacular blow-over accident during a morning race-day test run. Rookie driver John Walters suffered several injuries, including a fractured left hip socket and sprains of his left shoulder, elbow, and knee. (Courtesy of Bill Osborne.)

Bill Muncey set a competition lap record of 133.730 miles per hour to hold off Dean Chenoweth and the Griffon *Bud* to take a second straight Columbia Cup victory in 1980. The *Budweiser* was hampered by a malfunctioning nitrous oxide system and finished second. (Courtesy of Bill Osborne.)

Bill Bennett and Bill Pennington retired their traditional three-point *Miss Circus Circus* and experimented with a radical four-point design. A three-point boat rides on two forward sponsons and the propeller. A four-point boat rides on a single forward sponson, two rear sponsons, and the propeller. Designed by successful model racer Ed Fischer, the boat was driven by Ron Armstrong. It qualified for the Columbia Cup but was unable to finish a single heat. (Courtesy of Bill Osborne.)

The *Miss Budweiser* and the *Pay N' Pak* hooked up for a great duel in heat 2A until the *Pak* went dead in the water. (Courtesy of Bill Osborne.)

Chip Hanauer (seen here standing between Danny Walters (left) and Squire Shop crew chief Jerry Zuvich) was fast gaining a reputation as one of the better young drivers in the sport. (Courtesy of Bill Osborne.)

Even when Chip Hanauer's equipment was not as fast as his competitors, he could still find a way to win. In the final heat of the 1981 Columbia Cup, Dean Chenoweth in the *Miss Budweiser* thought he had a victory wrapped up and was coasting though the last lap. Chip caught Chenoweth in the final turn and ducked inside, beating Chenoweth to the finish by a matter of inches and "stealing" the win. (Courtesy of Bill Osborne.)

In the last race of the 1981 season, the world championship in Acapulco, Mexico, Bill Muncey was killed when his *Atlas Van Lines* crashed while leading the final heat. Bill's widow, Fran Muncey (left), and Atlas chairman O. H. Frisbie (right) struggled with how to proceed. Should they shut the team down or keep racing? Eventually they decided to keep going out of respect for Bill's love of the sport. They ordered a new boat from Jim Lucero and hired Chip Hanauer to drive. (Courtesy of Bill Osborne.)

Bernie Little (left) and Dean Chenoweth (right) were more then just employer/ employee, they were also good friends and had known each other for 12 years by 1982. Dean won the very first race he drove for Bernie in 1970, and of the 15 different drivers that had worked for Bernie up to 1982, Dean had won more races than the rest combined. (Courtesy of Bill Osborne.)

Dean Chenoweth was killed when the *Miss Budweiser* crashed while attempting to set a new Columbia Cup qualifying record on Saturday morning, July 31, 1982. Prior to this accident, drivers did not wear seatbelts, preferring to be thrown from a boat rather than sink to the bottom with the craft. When the damaged *Miss Budweiser* was brought back to the pits, it was clear that the cockpit was undamaged and that had Dean been strapped in, he most likely would have survived the accident.

Atlas crew chief and builder Jim Lucero and driver Chip Hanauer were the first to install seatbelts and a crash cockpit in an unlimited. The 1983 configuration of the *Atlas* (shown here) had a cockpit built to withstand significant impact. (Courtesy of Bill Osborne.)

This driver's-eye view of the front stretch of the Columbia Cup course shows the pits and the Blue Bridge, as seen by Ron Snyder as he takes a test lap in the *Frank Kenny Toyota Volvo* in 1983. (Courtesy of Bill Osborne.)

Jack Schafer Jr. surprised everybody when he drove Bob Taylor's *American Speedy Printing* to victory in the 1983 Columbia Cup. (Courtesy of Bill Osborne.)

Sixteen boats attempted to qualify for the 1984 Gold Cup in Tri-Cities, including future Gold Cup winner Mitch Evans in Rich Bowles's *Island Security Systems*. The boat failed to qualify. (Courtesy of Bill Osborne.)

Jerry Kenny unveiled his brand new *Frank Kenny Toyota Volvo* at the 1984 Gold Cup. The all-wood, Jon Staduacher–designed boat was powered by a turbocharged Allison engine and driven by Earle Hall. The boat finished 10th in her maiden race. (Courtesy of Bill Osborne.)

After winning two straight Gold Cups and national championships, the Atlas Van Lines team abandoned their tried and true Merlin engines and switched to a turbine engine. The new boat was fast but plagued by mechanical issues. They scored a tremendous come-from-behind victory in the 1984 Gold Cup. (Courtesy of Bill Osborne.)

Not only is Chip Hanauer a very talented race driver, but he has an amazing sense of humor. Here, to celebrate the first Gold Cup victory by a turbine-powered hydroplane, he poses with the trophy wearing a gold turban. (Courtesy of Bill Osborne.)

3

1985–1991

THE TURBINE YEARS

Turbine engines had been used in a number of different unlimited hydroplanes, dating back as early as 1969. John Walters recorded the first ever turbine victory when he drove the turbine-powered *Pay N' Pak* to first place at Thunder in the Park in Syracuse, New York, in 1982. There were no turbine boats at all in the 1983 unlimited fleet.

Nineteen hundred eighty-four saw the Atlas Van Lines, Lite All Star, and Tosti Asti teams all field turbine boats.

At the start of the 1985 season, there was still plenty of debate about what direction the future of the sport would take. Of the 14 teams preparing boats, only two were planning to run turbines—Fran Muncey's *Miller American* and Steve Woomer's *Miss 7 Eleven*.

The piston-powered forces were led by Bernie Little and the *Miss Budweiser*, who launched a brand new Rolls Royce Griffon–powered hull featuring a fully enclosed cockpit.

By the end of the 1985 season, the debate would be settled on the side of the turbines. Turbine-powered boats won six out of nine races and claimed the national championship. In fact, since 1985, a turbine-powered hydroplane has won every national championship, all but one Gold Cup, and all but one Columbia Cup!

When the unlimited fleet arrived in Tri-Cities for the 1985 Columbia Cup, they were treated to the sight of Chip Hanauer and the *Miller American* turning in a new 2.5-mile course record of 153.061 miles per hour! Chip went on to give Miller a perfect day, winning all three heats and claiming $15,655 in prize money. Bob Steil's *Squire Shop*, driven by Tom D'Eath, took second. Chip went on to win the 1985 national championship as well as his fourth straight Gold Cup.

Chip Hanauer and the Miller team came back to Tri-Cities in 1986 and repeated their performance, qualifying fastest and winning three straight heats; Tom D'Eath and the *Squire Shop* were again second. D'Eath complained loudly that Hanauer almost hit him in the second turn of the first lap of the final. "It's driving over your head and it's stupid," D'Eath said. "They have one set of rules for him and one set of rules for the rest of us." Hanauer downplayed the incident, saying "That's boat racing. He had an arc and I had an arc."

Jim Kropfeld won the national championship in a new turbine-powered *Miss Budweiser*, while Chip continued to collect Gold Cups, taking home an unprecedented fifth in a row.

In 1987, it was the *Budweiser*'s turn to win in Tri-Cities. A brand new turbine *Miss Budweiser*, driven by Jim Kropfeld, qualified fastest and won the race, as well as the national championship. Chip, however, continued his lock on the Gold Cup, winning it again in 1987.

Nineteen hundred eighty-eight was a banner year for the unlimiteds, with five different winners in the first five races of the season. *Oh Boy! Oberto* won in the season opener in Miami, the *Miller* won in Detroit, and then Chip claimed his seventh consecutive Gold Cup with the *Miss Circus Circus* in Evansville. *Mr. Pringles* won in Madison, and Tom D'Eath, who had taken over the *Miss Budweiser* cockpit after Jim Kropfeld was injured in Miami, won in Syracuse.

When the boats got to Tri-Cities, D'Eath and Hanauer continued to slug it out in the "Beer Wars." Chip and the *Miller High Life* won the qualifying battle, edging out the *Bud* with a lap of 153.296 miles per hour compared to D'Eath's 153.061. The *Miller* was damaged in the first heat and pulled out of the race. Fran Muncey asked Chip to drive the team's second boat, *Miss Circus Circus*, in the final. Hanauer and D'Eath locked up in an incredible battle with D'Eath and the *Bud* inching out a win by less then a second—the closest margin of victory in Columbia Cup history.

The 1989 Columbia Cup had a surprise ending worthy of Hollywood. Five of the top six qualifiers were turbine boats, and the fastest piston boat qualified almost 25 miles per hour slower than the fastest turbine. But as the philosophers say, "The race does not always go to the swiftest!" The *Miss Circus Circus* lost its rudder during prerace testing and had to withdraw, the *Pringles* flipped during a preliminary heat, and *US West* and *Winston Eagle* both had mechanical problems, leaving only the turbine-powered *Miss Budweiser* to battle the piston-powered boats. Tom D'Eath and the *Bud* were leading the final heat, when D'Eath washed down (sprayed with his roostertail) the third-place *Holset Miss Mazda* and was given a one-lap penalty, handing the victory to Ed Cooper's Allison-powered *Coopers Express*, driven by Mitch Evans. Later that year, Tom D'Eath finally broke Chip's stranglehold on the Gold Cup and claimed the trophy for Bernie Little and the *Miss Budweiser*.

The 1990 race featured a dramatic qualifying duel that saw three different boats bump up the course record no less than five times. By the morning of race day, Chip and the *Miss Circus Circus* sat atop the qualifying ladder with a speed of 156.866 miles per hour, Jim Kropfeld and the *Winston Eagle* were second on the ladder at 155.655 miles per hour, and Tom D'Eath was in third with the *Miss Budweiser* at 153.515 miles per hour. The race itself was anticlimatic when a combination of penalties and mechanical failures eliminated most of the top competitors and allowed D'Eath and the *Bud* to win in a walkaway.

The 1991 season saw driver changes at a number of top teams. Tom D'Eath was injured in a preseason car race and was replaced in the *Miss Budweiser* by Scott Pierce. Steve David stepped up to the U-2 when Mark Tate moved over to the *Winston Eagle* to replace Jim Kropfeld, the Circus team shutdown, and Chip Hanauer retired.

The 1991 Columbia Cup was a demolition derby. The *Miss Budweiser* and *Winston Eagle* collided in heat 2A, and the *Kellogg's Frosted Flakes* blew over on the third lap in the final and forced the race to be shortened. The victory went to Mark Tate and the battered but fast *Winston Eagle*.

Miss Budweiser crew chief Jeff Neff was Dean Chenoweth's brother-in-law, and when Dean was killed, Jeff vowed to make the sport safer. Jeff told *Budweiser*'s owner, Bernie Little, that if he was not allowed to build an enclosed cockpit for their new boat, he would resign. Bernie provided the funds, and Neff built the first fully enclosed safety cockpit. Jeff's sister (and Dean's widow) Jenny christened the new boat when it was launched. Between 1951 and 1982, there were 14 fatalities in unlimited racing. Since the introduction of the enclosed cockpit in 1985, there has been only one. (Courtesy of Bill Osborne.)

In 1985, Bernie Little launched a brand new Griffon-powered *Miss Budweiser*, designed and built by Ron Jones Sr. It was the third and final Griffon-powered *Miss Budweiser*. It won the Syracuse, New York, race early in the season and the San Diego race at the end, and was then retired and replaced by a turbine-powered boat. (Courtesy of Bill Osborne.)

Bob Gilliam returned to unlimited racing for three races in 1985 with the *Domino's Pizza*. With George Johnson at the wheel, this former *Miss Circus Circus* hull failed to qualify in Tri-Cities. (Courtesy of Bill Osborne.)

The former *Squire Shop* hull returned to action in 1985 as Jim Grader's *Tri-Cities Savings and Loan*, with Ron Snyder driving. Problems with the boat's turbocharged Allison engine kept it from qualifying. (Courtesy of Bill Osborne.)

Mitch Evans drove Fred Leland's Merlin-powered *Miss Rock* to seventh place in the 1985 Columbia Cup. (Courtesy of Bill Osborne.)

Jim Kropfeld and the *Miss Budweiser* battle with Andy Cooker in the *American Speedy Printing* in heat 1A of the 1985 Columbia Cup. (Courtesy of Bill Osborne.)

At the 1985 Columbia Cup, Steve Reynolds was the second-fastest qualifier with Steve Woomer's *Miss 7 Eleven*. The boat won its first heat and looked to be a real contender, but back-to-back mechanical breakdowns dropped her to fourth place. (Courtesy of Bill Osborne.)

Chip Hanauer and the *Miller American* qualified nine miles an hour faster than any other boat and won all three heats to claim the trophy. Tom D'Eath in the *Squire Shop* took second place. (Courtesy of Bill Osborne.)

Under the white, blue, orange, and red of the *Frank Kenny Toyota Volvo* was a heart of Budweiser gold. This hull, originally the three-time national champion Griffon *Budweiser*, returned to racing in 1986 with a turbocharged Allison in the engine compartment and Milner Irvine in the cockpit. They finished fourth in the Columbia Cup. (Courtesy of Bill Osborne.)

Future Gold Cup winner Mike Hanson made his unlimited debut in Fred Leland's all-white *Boat* for the 1986 Columbia Cup. (Courtesy of Bill Osborne.)

Bernie Little (left) and Steve Woomer (center) became great friends during their many years racing together. Here Little and Woomer pose in front of the *Miss 7 Eleven* with driver Steve Reynolds. (Courtesy of Bill Osborne.)

At the start of heat 2A in the 1986 Columbia Cup, the *Mr. Pringles*, *Miller American*, and *Squire Shop* all hit the line together. Chip went on to win the heat and the race. (Courtesy of Bob Greenhow.)

Jim Kropfeld drove the turbine-powered *Miss Budweiser* to three victories and a national championship in 1986. (Courtesy of F. Pierce Williams.)

Chip and the *Miller American* won five races in 1986, but their failure to score any points in the two saltwater races knocked them out of the high points chase. (Courtesy of Bill Osborne.)

At the end of the 1986 season, Bob Steil sold the entire U-2 Squire Shop race team to longtime crew chief Jim Harvey. The team's transport truck caught fire on their way to the race in Miami, and their entire inventory of six motors, along with most of the tools and support gear, were destroyed. The boat escaped serious damage, and the team rebounded with a fourth-place finish in the Columbia Cup. (Courtesy of Bill Osborne.)

Todd Yarling drove Jim Sedam's turbocharged, Allison-powered *Pietro's Pizza* to sixth place in Tri-Cities in 1986. (Courtesy of Bill Osborne.)

1985–1991: THE TURBINE YEARS

Bill Wurster and crew chief Dan Heye converted the Rolls Royce Merlin–powered *Mr. Pringles* to turbine power for the 1987 season. They won in Detroit and took third place in the Columbia Cup with Scott Pierce driving. (Courtesy of Bill Osborne.)

In 1987, *Frank Kenny Toyota Volvo* swapped their turbocharged Allison for a turbocharged Rolls Royce Griffon and captured fifth place in the Columbia Cup. (Courtesy of Bill Osborne.)

A brand new *Miller American* gave Chip and the rest of the Miller team fits for the first half of the 1987. Try as they might, they could not break into the winner's circle. The old boat was brought out of retirement after Seattle and allowed Chip to win the final two races of the season, including his sixth straight Gold Cup. (Courtesy of Bill Osborne.)

A new *Miss Budweiser* was launched in 1987. The boat's career got off to an inauspicious start when it blew over in Seattle on the very first lap of its initial test run. Driver Jim Kropfeld was uninjured, thanks to the new enclosed cockpit. The boat was repaired in time to win five of the first six races in 1987, including the Columbia Cup. (Courtesy of Bill Osborne.)

Jim Kropfeld was seriously injured in the final heat of the first race of the 1988 season. He was driving the *Miss Budweiser* when she hooked and was run over by the *Mr. Pringles*. Jim sustained a broken neck and was replaced in the cockpit by Tom D'Eath. D'Eath went on to win four races and the national championship. (Courtesy of Bill Osborne.)

Competition was fierce in 1988, with five different boats winning the first five races. *Oh Boy! Oberto* won the season opener in Miami, Chip and the *Miller* won in Detroit, Chip drove the *Miss Circus Circus* to victory in the Gold Cup, *Mr. Pringles* won in Madison, and D'Eath and the *Budweiser* took home the trophy from the Syracuse race. (Courtesy of Bill Osborne.)

In 1988, Steve Woomer's boat showed off a new name and paint scheme for Tri-Cities, and the U-10 was sponsored by R. J. Reynolds Vantage Ultra cigarettes. Larry Lauterbach drove the boat to a fourth-place finish. (Courtesy of Bill Osborne.)

Chuck Hickling spent several years trying to get his experimental Merlin-powered tunnel hull to work. Jack Schaffer qualified the boat at 103.675 miles per hour for the 1988 Columbia Cup but failed to score any points. (Courtesy of Bill Osborne.)

The *Miss Madison* team launched their brand new boat at the 1988 Columbia Cup. The new Ron Jones–built boat was powered by a turbocharged Allison and ran under the name *Holset Miss Madison* with Ron Snyder driving. (Courtesy of Bill Osborne.)

Fran Muncey ran a two-boat team in 1988. The *Miss Circus Circus* was driven by John Prevost and the *Miller High Life* was driven by Chip Hanauer. Chip had much more experience than Prevost and would occasionally replace him in the *Circus* cockpit. Chip drove the *Circus* to victory in the final heat of the Gold Cup in Evansville and just barely lost to Tom D'Eath and the *Miss Budweiser* in a dramatic final-heat battle at the Columbia Cup. (Courtesy of Bill Osborne.)

Some drivers are able to fight hard during a race but remain friends on the beach. Chip Hanauer and Tom D'Eath were not like that. They had a fierce rivalry both on and off the racecourse. Here the *Bud* and the *Miller* scream into the first turn of heat 1A of the 1988 Columbia Cup. Tom won the heat, the race, and the national championship. (Courtesy of Bill Osborne.)

Tom D'Eath (left), Bernie Little (center), and crew chief Ron Brown celebrate their 1988 Columbia Cup victory. Tom and Ron had a long history, going back to the days of the Miss U.S. racing team; Ron was crew chief for the *Miss U.S.* when Tom won the 1976 Gold Cup. Ron was also crew chief on the *Lite All Star*, which Tom drove for Bob Taylor in 1984. (Courtesy of Bill Osborne.)

1985–1991: THE TURBINE YEARS

Scott Pierce and the *Mr. Pringles* had a rough time in the 1989 season, crashing three times in five races, including the Columbia Cup. (Courtesy of Bill Osborne.)

The three-race Vantage Ultra sponsorship from R. J. Reynolds in 1988 grew into a full-circuit Winston Eagle sponsorship for Steve Woomers's U-10 in 1989. (Courtesy of Bill Osborne.)

The primary *Miss Circus Circus* hull was badly damaged in a blow over accident two weeks before the 1989 Columbia Cup. The backup hull was activated and looked fast until she lost a rudder race-day morning and had to withdraw. (Courtesy of Bill Osborne.)

Tom D'Eath and the *Miss Budweiser* were penalized one lap when they cut off Mike Hanson and the *Holset Miss Mazda* late in the final heat of the 1989 Columbia Cup. The penalty knocked the *Budweiser* from first place to third place, allowing Mitch Evans in the *Coopers Express* to win and the *Holset Miss Mazda*, shown here racing the *Oh Boy! Oberto*, to take home second place. (Courtesy of Bill Osborne.)

In 1990, the *Oh Boy! Oberto* was set up to run either the Rolls Royce Merlin or the Lycoming turbine engine. Turbine motors have difficulty running on saltwater racecourses, so the *Oberto* tried to use the Merlin engine at Miami and San Diego where the race took place in saltwater and the Lycoming at all other races. (Courtesy of Bill Osborne.)

At the end of the 1988 season, Fran Muncey sold her entire race team to Bill Bennett, who owned Circus Circus casinos. Bennett kept Hanauer as the driver and hired Dave Villwock to be crew chief. They won six races and the 1990 national championship. (Courtesy of Bill Osborne.)

Tom D'Eath and the *Miss Budweiser* won five races in 1990, including the Gold Cup and the Columbia Cup. (Courtesy of Bill Osborne.)

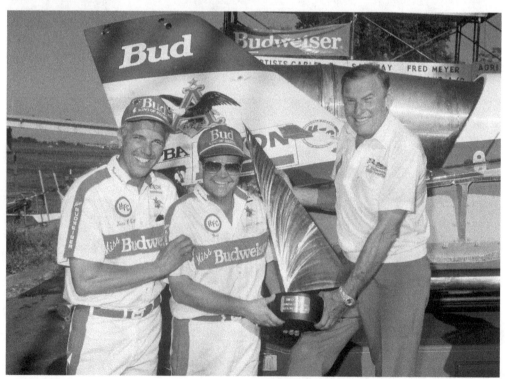

Tom D'Eath, Ron Brown, and Bernie Little celebrate their 1990 Columbia Cup victory. The team of D'Eath, Brown, and Little won 12 out of 25 races that they entered between 1988 and 1990. (Courtesy of Bill Osborne.)

Even though the Lycoming turbine engine was dominating the sport, innovative owners continued to experiment with other power plants. Mike and Larry Rutkauskas of Tri-Cities campaigned the automotive-powered former *Miss Renault* as *The Edge*, sponsored by Edge Shaving Gel. (Courtesy of Bill Osborne.)

The 1989 Columbia Cup winner returned in 1990 sponsored by Oh Boy! Oberto and Wild Waves Water Park. They finished sixth place. (Courtesy of Bill Osborne.)

Bill Wurster's U-8 ran as *Super Range Golf* in the 1991 Columbia Cup with George Woods handling the driving duties. (Courtesy of Bill Osborne.)

Ron Jones Jr., grandson of Ted Jones, the man credited with designing the first successful prop-riding unlimited hydroplane, entered the hydro wars with the U-50 *American Spirit*, driven by Mark Evans. The U-50 was a four-time Gold Cup winner that had been built in 1984 as the *Atlas Van Lines*. Evans and Jones won the 1991 Indiana Governor's Cup in Madison, Indiana, and finished fifth in the Columbia Cup that year. (Courtesy of Bill Osborne.)

Future unlimited commissioner Ken Muscatel made his unlimited debut at the Columbia Cup in 1991 driving Bob Fendler's *Jackpot Food Mart*. Ken earned an eighth-place finish and Rookie of the Year honors. (Courtesy of Bill Osborne.)

Bernie Little was expecting Tom D'Eath to drive the *Miss Budweiser* in 1991, but just before the start of the season, D'Eath was hurt in a stock car race. Little quickly hired Scott Pierce to take over. Pierce won the national championship for Little, but because the points from a race in Honolulu in November 1990 were included in the point totals for 1991, Mark Tate, driving the *Winston Eagle*, had more driver's points and claimed the driving title. (Courtesy of Bill Osborne.)

The 1991 Columbia Cup was a "good news, bad news" event for the *Miss Madison* team. They started the weekend by announcing that they had landed a major national sponsorship and that the boat would now be called *Kellogg's Frosted Flakes*. However, on the third lap of the final heat, Mike Hanson blew the boat over causing the race to be stopped. (Courtesy of Bill Osborne.)

Mark Tate and the *Winston Eagle* won three races in 1991—the Gold Cup in Detroit, the Columbia Cup in Tri-Cities, and the Top Gun Hydro Fest in Honolulu. Mark Tate also claimed the driving title, edging out Scott Pierce by less than 600 points. (Courtesy of Bill Osborne.)

4

1992 – 1999

THE BUDWEISER YEARS

No single unlimited owner has had a greater impact on the Tri-Cities race than Lakeland, Florida's, Bernie Little. Little, who owned the *Miss Budweiser* from 1964 until his death in 2003, won the very first Atomic Cup in 1966 and went on to win the Tri-Cities race 10 more times. His son, Joe Little, won in 2004.

Bernie's influence was not just limited to winning races. Bernie was instrumental in forging a strong relationship between the Water Follies and Anheuser-Busch (the brewers of Budweiser beer). Because of Bernie's influence, Budweiser began sponsoring the race in 1984 and did not stop until 2006. There were times when it seemed like just about every aspect of unlimited racing was sponsored by Anheuser-Busch. For example, in 1992, seven out of nine races were sponsored by Budweiser, and the national championship was sponsored by Eagle Snacks, a division of Anheuser-Busch. Many people argued that this type of single-sponsor domination was bad for the sport. Others claim that Bernie kept the sport afloat during difficult times. Either way, he left his imprint on the sport in a way that will never be equaled.

Bernie Little started the 1992 season by luring Chip Hanauer out of retirement to drive the *Miss Budweiser*. Fans were anxious to see what would happen when the best driver in the sport got a chance to drive the best equipment in the sport. What happened was total domination! Chip and the *Miss Budweiser* won their first five races, including a perfect sweep in the Columbia Cup, qualifying fastest and winning all four heats. Chip and the *Bud* won seven out of nine races that year, including the Gold Cup and the national championship.

Chip and the *Bud* continued to dominate the field in 1993, winning seven out of 10 races, including the Gold Cup and the Columbia Cup.

Chip was injured at the start of the 1994 season when the escape hatch on the bottom of *Miss Budweiser* came open during the Gold Cup in Detroit. The blast of water broke four of Chip's vertebrae and put him on the sidelines for two races. He was back in the boat for Tri-Cities and swept the Columbia Cup with a perfect weekend—qualifying fastest and winning all of his heats—for the third time in three years.

Chip and the *Bud*'s stranglehold on the Columbia Cup ended in 1995 when Mark Tate and the *Smokin' Joe's* qualified fastest and beat the *Budweiser* in four straight heats to claim the trophy.

Chip retired from the Budweiser team after an accident in the 1996 Gold Cup, and Mark Evans took over the ride. Fred Leland's *PICO American Dream*, driven by Dave Villwock, won the Gold Cup and the Columbia Cup on their way to a national championship.

Evans and Villwock swapped rides for 1997; Villwock left the *PICO* to take over the *Budweiser* cockpit, and Evans left the *Budweiser* and moved back to the *PICO*. Villwock started off the 1997 season with five straight wins and was well on his way to a sixth when the *Miss Budweiser* flipped and landed upside down and backwards while leading the field out of the first turn of the final heat in Tri-Cities. The impact of the accident caved in the back of the *Budweiser*'s cockpit, ripped off Villwock's helmet, and nearly amputated his right hand.

Unlimited Racing Commission (URC) rescue diver Mark Allen, the first diver to reach Villwock, said, "It was a mess under there! It was bloody and the water was murky too. I felt for his head, and he didn't have his helmet on, so I put my hand on his face to see if his oxygen mask was on, it wasn't!" Allen and the rest of the URC rescue team extricated the unconscious Villwock from the wreckage and revived him before he was airlifted to Seattle. Two fingers on his right hand were amputated, and followers of the sport feared that his promising career was over.

With the *Budweiser* out of the race, Mark Evans and the *PICO American Dream* won the restart of the race.

Villwock surprised everyone and returned to the *Budweiser* cockpit in 1998, winning 8 out of 10 races, including the Gold Cup. He had a perfect weekend at the Columbia Cup, qualifying fastest and winning every heat. He also claimed the national championship.

As the 1999 season neared, Villwock and the *Miss Budweiser* seemed unbeatable, so Fred Leland lured Chip Hanauer out of retirement with what Chip referred to as "an obscene amount of money!" Chip and the *PICO* won three of the first five races in 1999, and as the boats came to Tri-Cities for the Columbia Cup, Chip was poised to tie Bill Muncey's career record of 62 victories.

Chip was not really comfortable with his motivation for driving the *PICO*. He had already won 61 races and 11 Gold Cups and did not need to prove anything to anybody. "I was only driving for the money and that didn't really feel right. I kept thinking, 'What happens if I crash and end up paralyzed? What good will the money do me then?'"

As the race unfolded, both Chip and Dave won their first two preliminary heats and were drawn together for heat 3A. As the boats roared out of the second turn, the *PICO* became airborne and began to flip. "I can remember hanging upside down," Chip recalls and thinking, "Great, this is it! I'm going to end up paralyzed, because I was too greedy!"

The boat landed upside down and then flopped right side up. "The first thing I did was wiggle my fingers and toes. Once I knew everything worked I stared to laugh! I knew it was all over, I'd made it through alive and in one piece and it was time to retire!"

Villwock went on to win the race, and Hanauer retired.

Procter and Gamble (PG) returned to unlimited racing in 1992. PG had sponsored Bill Wurster's *Mr. Pringles* in the late 1980s and returned to the sport by sponsoring Wurster's *Tide*. George Woods drove the boat to second place in the Columbia Cup, Gold Cup, and national high points. (Courtesy of Bill Osborne.)

Mark Evans took fifth place in the Columbia Cup with Ron Jones Jr.'s *American Spirit/Pietro's Pizza*. Rookie Nate Brown drove Fred Leland's *Miss Rock* to sixth place and impressed enough people along the way to win Rookie of the Year. (Courtesy of Bill Osborne.)

Mark Tate and the *Winston Eagle* were fast in 1992 but were plagued by mechanical problems and finished third in Tri-Cities and third in the national high points standings. (Courtesy of Bill Osborne.)

The combination of Hanauer and the *Miss Budweiser* were unstoppable in 1992, winning seven out of nine races, including the Gold Cup and Columbia Cup, on their way to the 1992 national championship. Hanauer was initially reluctant to drive for Bernie Little. He was concerned that having the sport's two biggest names on the same team would be bad for competition. It was only after he became convinced that Mark Tate and the *Winston Eagle* would be formidable competitors that he agreed to take the job. (Courtesy of Bill Osborne.)

Jim McBride and Jack Barrie were ready to give up on the idea of piston power. They attempted to qualify the *Miss Tubs* with a Griffon engine at Tri-Cities in 1993. They did not succeed. (Courtesy of Bill Osborne.)

The 1993 Columbia Cup looked like a demolition derby, with almost every boat sustaining some type of damage. Mark Evans lost the cowlings, tail fins, and horizontal stabilizer from Fred Leland's U-100 *American Spirit*, but continued to race, taking fourth place overall. (Courtesy of Bill Osborne.)

Mike Jones, Ken Muscatel, and Bob Thomas formed Superior Racing to run the U-55 *Miss Wicked*, sponsored by Pete's Wicked Ale. Muscatel and Jones alternated driving duties. Jones captured seventh place at the 1993 Columbia Cup. (Courtesy of Bill Osborne.)

Chip and the *Budweiser* continued to dominate, winning 7 out of 10 races and sweeping the Columbia Cup for the second year in a row. (Courtesy of Bill Osborne.)

Mike Eacrett blew the *Oh Boy! Oberto* over attempting to qualify for the 1994 Columbia Cup. (Courtesy of Chris Denslow.)

Eacrett was not seriously injured, but the boat was completely destroyed. (Courtesy of Chris Denslow.)

Glen Davis's experimental four-point hydro was sponsored by Ellstrom Manufacturing and driven by Ken Dryden. The radical craft did not make it into the Columbia Cup and crashed violently the following week in Seattle. (Courtesy of Bill Osborne.)

Nate Brown drove Bill Wurster's *Tide/Taco Time* to fourth place in the 1994 Columbia Cup. (Courtesy of Bill Osborne.)

The *Miss Exide*, driven by Mira Slovak, was very popular in 1963. More than 30 years later, Exide returned to the sport of unlimited racing in 1994 with a two-boat team. Mark Evans drove the *Miss Exide*, and Jimmy King drove the *Miss Exide II*. (Courtesy of Bill Osborne.)

Robb Thompson owned the new Exide team. Here, from left to right, Robb poses with Mark Evans, Jimmy King, and former *Miss Exide* driver Mira Slovak in front of the *Miss Exide*. (Courtesy of Bill Osborne.)

In 1994, the Budweiser team replaced the familiar gold, white, and red paint scheme with a new all-red look that matched the appearance of the Budweiser drag car and other Budweiser-sponsored vehicles. The paint scheme did not seem to matter as Chip and the *Bud* continued to rack up national championships in 1994 and 1995. (Courtesy of Bill Osborne.)

The U-6 had a split personality in 1995, spending the first half of the season painted green and called *Jasper Engines and Transmissions* and the second half of the season painted yellow and called *DeWalt Tools*. Mike Hanson drove the boat to sixth place in national high points. (Courtesy of Bill Osborne.)

Dave Villwock moved to the U-100 *PICO American Dream* in 1994. They finished the season with back-to-back wins in Seattle and San Diego. Even though they did not win any races in 1995, they were consistently in the final heat and captured third place in national high points that year. (Courtesy of Bill Osborne.)

Villwock started his boat-racing career when he was only 16 years old. He was particularly successful in the Flatbottom and Cracker Box classes and won his first national championship when he was 20. By the time he began driving unlimiteds in 1992, he already had over 20 years experience as a driver. (Courtesy of Bill Osborne.)

Mark Tate and the *Smokin' Joe's* won four races in 1995, including a perfect sweep of the Columbia Cup. (Courtesy of Bill Osborne.)

Steve Woomer and Mark Tate accept the Columbia Cup trophy from 1995 Tri City queen Jamie Robinson. Even though the *Miss Budweiser* won the 1994 and 1995 High Point Championship, Mark Tate, driving the *Smokin' Joe's*, won the 1994 and 1995 Driver's Championship because Chip Hanauer had been replaced in the *Budweiser* cockpit at a couple of races each season due to injuries. (Courtesy of Bill Osborne.)

In 1996, Bob Fendler's U-19 picked up a significant sponsorship from the high-tech firm Appian Graphics to promote their Jeronimo video cards. The *Appian Jeronimo* was driven by Spokane's Tom Hindley.

The *Appian Jeronimo* blew over and crashed violently in the provisional heat of the 1996 Columbia Cup. Hindley escaped serious injury when the cockpit failed and broke in half. (Courtesy of Bill Osborne.)

The Ellstroms continued to struggle with their new boat. They attended only two races and got a pair of ninth-place finishes. (Courtesy of Bill Osborne.)

Chip Hanauer retired after he was injured when the *Miss Budweiser* and the *Smoking Joe's* collided in the Gold Cup in Detroit. Mark Evans was hired to replace him. (Courtesy of Bill Osborne.)

1992–1999: THE BUDWEISER YEARS

Budweiser took sixth at the Columbia Cup. Most fans thought that the big story of the day was that Villwock and the *PICO* had defeated the *Budweiser*. They were wrong. While wading in the river, Will Thomas, a fan, stumbled on what he thought was a rock, but when he pulled it from the river, he realized it was a human skull! Not wanting to miss the final heat, he stashed it under some bushes. After the race, he turned the skull over to a Benton County sheriff deputy. Eventually, the skull was identified as being 9,000 years old. Named "Kennewick Man," the skull is considered to be one of the most important anthropological finds ever made in North America. (Courtesy of Mark Hooton.)

Dave Villwock and the *PICO* dominated the 1996 season, winning 6 out of 10 races, including the Gold Cup, Columbia Cup, and the national championship. Fans were optimistic that Villwock and Leland would be able to overthrow the Budweiser dynasty and restore long-term competition to the sport. It was not to be. Bernie Little quickly hired Dave Villwock to replace the retiring Hanauer, and the Budweiser dynasty just continued to roll. (Courtesy of Bill Osborne.)

Dr. Ken Muscatel drove the U-14 *Computers and Applications* to a 12th place finish at the 1997 Columbia Cup. (Courtesy of Bill Osborne.)

Mitch Evans spent most of his unlimited career driving a turbocharged Allison boat, but he stepped into the turbine-powered *Appian Jeronimo* after Tom Hindley was injured in 1996 and placed sixth in the 1997 Columbia Cup. (Courtesy Mark Hooton.)

Dave Villwock was seriously injured when the *Miss Budweiser* blew over on the first lap of the final heat of the 1997 Columbia Cup. The boat landed upside down and backwards, caving in the cockpit, ripping Villwock's helmet off, and almost amputating his right hand. Villowock was unconscious and not breathing when rescue divers arrived on the scene. Rescue workers were able to revive him, and he was airlifted to Seattle, but two of his fingers had to be amputated.

Mark Evans in the *PICO American Dream* was able to capitalize on the *Budweiser* team's misfortune and won four of the last six races of the season. (Courtesy of Bill Osborne.)

For years, the original *Miss Tri-Cities* sat atop a pole at the entrance of Columbia Park. She was taken down in 1994 when she began to look old and dilapidated. A group of model boat racers converted a 1980s vintage automotive-powered boat to look like a turbine and installed it on a new pole in 1998. (Courtesy of Chris Denslow.)

Fred Leland launched his brand new U-7 *United Furniture Warehouse* at the 1998 Columbia Cup. The new boat, driven by Rick Christensen and rookie Greg Hopp, finished 10th. (Courtesy of Bill Osborne.)

Nate Brown drove Bill Wurster's *Llumar Window Film Presents Miss Tri-Cities* to second place at the 1998 Columbia Cup. Llumar would become a full-circuit sponsor for Wurster the following year. (Courtesy of Bill Osborne.)

The U-16 *Miss Elam Plus* continued to improve every year and captured a third-place finish at the 1998 Columbia Cup with Jimmy King driving. (Courtesy of Bill Osborne.)

In 1998, Jerry Hale qualified Bob Fendler's *Easter Seals* at 146 miles per hour and took seventh place in Tri-Cities. (Courtesy of Bill Osborne.)

When Dave Villwock lost part of his hand in the vicious *Miss Budweiser* crash in 1997, most of the experts predicted that his career as a boat driver was over. Villwock proved the so-called experts wrong by coming back and dominating the 1998 season. He won 8 out of 10 races, including the Gold Cup, the Columbia Cup, and the national championship. (Courtesy of Bill Osborne.)

Greg Hopp drove the 1999
version of the *Miss Tri-
Cities* to a fourth-place
finish in the Columbia Cup.
(Courtesy of Bill Osborne.)

Lawrence Wisne, the owner
and chief executive officer
of Progressive Tool and
Industries Inc. (PICO),
wanted to beat Villwock
and the *Miss Budweiser,* and
he was willing to pay Chip
Hanauer "whatever it took" to
entice him out of retirement
and drive for PICO. Chip
responded by winning his
11th Gold Cup and taking
first place in three of the first
five races in 1999. (Courtesy
of F. Pierce Williams.)

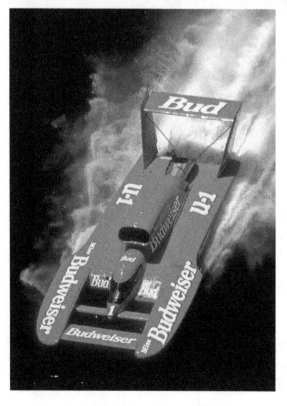

Chip retired after the *PICO* blew over backwards and crashed during the third heat of the 1999 Columbia Cup. Chip had 61 race wins to his credit and was only one win away from tying the record 62 wins, held by his mentor Bill Muncey. (Courtesy of Bill Osborne.)

With Hanauer out of the way, Villwock was not seriously challenged for the rest of 1999, winning the last six races of the season. (Courtesy F. Pierce Williams.)

5

2 0 0 0 – 2 0 0 7

THE ELAM YEARS

By its very nature, Gold Cup and unlimited racing is prone to dynasties. In the early days, Gar Wood won the Gold Cup five years in a row, between 1917 and 1921. In the 1930s, *El Lagarto* won the cup three straight years. In the early 1950s, Stan Sayres and his *Slo-mo-shun* boats won the cup five times in five years. In the mid-1960s, Ole Bardahl and his *Miss Bardahl* won the Gold Cup and national championship five times in six years. Between 1982 and 1988, Chip Hanauer won the cup seven times. Bernie Little won the national championship five times in a row between 1991 and 1995, and then eight more times between 1997 and 2004. Dynasties are just part of the racing landscape.

When Budweiser left the sport at the end of the 2004 season, it was only natural that some other team would rise up and create a new dynasty. That team was Ellstrom Manufacturing and their *Miss Elam Plus*.

Ellstrom entered the sport in 1994, when they sponsored Glenn Davis's reverse four-point hydro. The experimental craft crashed attempting to qualify for the Seattle Seafair race, and driver Ken Dryden was seriously injured. Ellstrom returned with a brand-new boat, built from Fred Leland's molds, in 1995. The team struggled for their first five years but hit their stride at the 2000 Columbia Cup.

Dave Villwock and the *Miss Budweiser* came to the 2000 Columbia Cup riding a 10-race victory streak that had started at the Columbia Cup in 1999. Villwock qualified fastest and won his first preliminary heat, but in his second heat, he was involved in a collision that badly damaged his right sponson, and he was forced to withdraw from the race. Mark Evans in *Miss Elam Plus* won the final heat to give the Ellstrom family their first victory.

In 2001, the Ellstrom team launched a new boat, built by Dale VanWieringen. Mark Evans took a job doing color commentary for ESPN, so Nate Brown stepped into the *Elam*'s cockpit.

Fred Leland ran two boats for his new sponsor Znetix, with Greg Hopp driving one boat and rookie Terry Troxell driving the second boat. Dave Villwock and the *Miss Budweiser* won the opening race of the season and came into Tri-Cities with great expectations. It was not to be. In a textbook example of team driving, Troxell and Hopp both started inside of Villwock in the final heat. While Hopp kept Villwock busy, forcing him wide in every turn, Troxell and the *Znetix II* built a commanding lead and won easily. *Elam* finished a distant fifth after Brown got a very late start.

Nate Brown made up for his disappointing performance in the Columbia Cup final by winning the next weekend in Seattle and following that up with a win in San Diego.

At the 2002 Columbia Cup, Nate Brown and *Miss Elam Plus* beat out the *Miss Budweiser* to qualify fastest, setting a new record at 162.666 miles per hour. In the final heat, the two boats hooked up in a tremendous struggle that lasted for three laps, until the *Budweiser* slipped into *Elam*'s rooster tail and almost blew over. It was only a masterful driving job on the part of Villwock that averted an accident. Unfortunately, while Villwock was trying to save the flying *Budweiser*, he cut inside a buoy and was disqualified. Brown went on to win easily.

Bernie Little passed away in the spring of 2003, but his son Joe stepped up to take over the reigns of the Budweiser race team. This hard-fought season saw the reemergence of a competitive piston-powered boat, when the U-3, owned by Ed Cooper Jr., won two of the first three races, including the Detroit Gold Cup. Mark Evans drove Bill Wurster's U-8 *Llumar* to a very popular victory at the 2003 Columbia Cup. The final heat was a wild and woolly shoot-out that saw plenty of bumping and banging. Over half of the final-heat field returned to the pits after the race with noticeable damage.

Prior to the start of the season, Joe Little announced that 2004 would be the last year of racing for the *Miss Budweiser*. Their Columbia Cup swan song was a runaway victory where Villwock and the *Miss Budweiser* qualified fastest and won all four heats. It was somehow appropriate that the *Miss Budweiser* would win the very first time she raced in Tri-Cities and the very last time she raced in Tri-Cities.

The 2005 season started with J. W. Meyer in the cockpit of the *Miss Elam Plus*. J. W. won the second race of the year in Madison, Indiana, but was unceremoniously fired after he blew the boat over attempting to qualify for the Gold Cup in Detroit. When the boats arrived in Tri-Cities, eight-time driving champion Dave Villwock was behind the wheel. Villwock and the *Elam* quickly showed the racing world that they were a force to be reckoned with as they qualified fastest and swept the field to win the race. They won again in San Diego and clinched their first national championship as a team.

Two thousand and six saw Villwock and the *Elam Plus* on the winner's podium again, but this time they had to perform a miracle. In a preliminary heat, the *Elam* went end over end in a spectacular blow over accident. Ellstrom's amazing crew somehow was able to repair the boat in time for the final heat, and Villwock made a perfect start and drove away to victory.

In 2007, the *Elam* swept the Columbia Cup again, setting a new qualifying record and winning all four heats. Villwock and the *Elam* also won the Gold Cup and the national championship, making it the team's most successful year in the sport.

The big boats have been coming to Tri-Cities for over 40 years, and the race is such a big part of the region's identity, it is easy to imagine that they will continue for another 40.

George Straton took second place in the 2000 Columbia Cup driving Kim Gregory's U-5 *Appian Jeronimo*. Stratton was a rookie in unlimited racing but had many years' experience in limited boats. He was killed less then two months later when the *Appian* blew over during a morning test run before the San Diego race. (Courtesy of Bill Osborne.)

The *Miss Budweiser* was severely damaged in a chain-reaction accident at the start of its second heat in the 2000 Columbia Cup. Villwock and the *Miss Budweiser* had to withdraw from the rest of the day's competition. (Courtesy of Chris Denslow.)

Mark Evans drove the *Miss Elam* to victory at the 2000 Columbia Cup, giving the Ellstrom family their first unlimited victory. (Courtesy of Bill Osborne.)

Eric Ellstrom and Mark Evans celebrate with the 2000 Columbia Cup trophy. (Courtesy of Bill Osborne.)

The Ellstrom team made a number of changes preparing for the 2001 season. Mark Evans was replaced in the cockpit by Nate Brown, and their old boat was replaced by a new boat, built by Dale VanWieringen, a former *Miss Budweiser* crew member. The new *Miss Elam* was very fast, but a poor start by Brown in the final heat cost them a chance at victory. Brown more than made up for his Tri-Cities mistake by winning the following weekend in Seattle and then in San Diego. (Courtesy of Bill Osborne.)

In the middle of the 2000 season, the American Power Boat Association turned over control of all unlimited racing to a new organization called Hydro-Prop. One of Hydro-Prop's goals was to establish parity on the racecourse. They attempted to do this by placing restrictions on all of the boats, but the Budweiser team received the harshest restrictions. In 2001, the *Budweiser* was only able to win the opening race of the season, but they still managed to claim a fifth straight national championship. (Courtesy of Bill Osborne.)

Starting in 2000, Fred Leland's team had the backing of a mysterious new company named Znetix. No one was ever able to say for sure what business Znetix was in. Eventually the company was closed by the Securities and Exchange Commission and the founders arrested for stock fraud. (Courtesy of Bill Osborne.)

Terry Troxell drove the *Znetix II* to victory at the 2001 Columbia Cup. Even though Troxell got the trophy, it was truly a team victory with Greg Hopp in the *Znetix* keeping Dave Villwock and the *Miss Budweiser* busy for several laps so that Troxell could build a commanding lead. (Courtesy of Bill Osborne.)

The final heat of the 2002 Columbia Cup featured a dramatic battle between Nate Brown in the *Miss Elam Plus* and Dave Villwock in the *Miss Budweiser*. The two boats raced side by side for three straight laps until the *Bud* slipped into the *Elam*'s roostertail. The *Bud* rode up the *Elam*'s fin water and almost blew over. Only a driver with Dave Villwock's skill could have saved the boat from crashing. However, while Villwock was struggling to bring the boat back under control, he cut inside the course and was disqualified. Brown went on to win the race and earned the Ellstrom family their second Columbia Cup trophy in three years. (Courtesy of Bill Osborne.)

Nate Brown and the *Elam* crew celebrate on the victory stand after winning the 2001 Columbia Cup. (Courtesy of Bill Osborne.)

Ken Muscatel's U-25 was sponsored by Silver Dollar Casinos in 2002. (Courtesy of Bill Osborne.)

The 2002 Columbia Cup was just about over—the lead boats had crossed the finish line and were slowing down—when Muscatel's *Silver Dollar Casino* blew over backwards and literally broke in half. Muscatel was not hurt and leased one of Fred Leland's backup boats to race the next week in Seattle. (Courtesy of Bill Osborne.)

Ken Maurer was one of the original five Water Follies board members. Eventually his advertising agency, the Maurer Group, would take over day-to-day operations of the Water Follies. Maurer retired in 2003 after devoting the better part of four decades to the race. (Courtesy of Tri-Cities Water Follies.)

In 2002, Ed Cooper had a new boat built with the help of Dale VanWieringen. The turbocharged, Allison-powered U-3 turned heads in San Diego when it qualified at over 160 miles per hour. In 2003, they won the Gold Cup in Detroit and took third place in the Columbia Cup. (Courtesy of Bill Osborne.)

Mark Evans and the U-8 *Llumar* not only outraced the competition in the 2003 Columbia Cup, they out-survived the competition. The U-8 prevailed in a final heat that saw plenty of bumping and banging, tempers flaring, and accusations made, but in the end, the results stood, and Bill Wurster and Mark Evans took the trophy home. (Courtesy of Bill Osborne.)

From left to right, Mark Evans, crew chief Scott Raney, and boat owner Bill Wurster celebrate with the 2003 Columbia Cup trophy. (Courtesy of Bill Osborne.)

Jim Harvey's U-2 was sponsored by Rob Graham and called *Miss Graham Trucking*. Rob Graham, a native of the Northwest, grew up watching and loving the hydros. Over the years, he has been a big supporter of hydroplane racing, sponsoring a number of limited and unlimited boats. (Courtesy of Bill Osborne.)

Rookie J. Michael Kelly was chosen to drive Jim Harvey's *Miss Graham Trucking*. Kelly was well known in the outboard classes but did not have much experience in the limited inboards that are normally the training ground for unlimited drivers. Kelly impressed unlimited fans immediately with his great starts and good boat sense. Kelly was voted Rookie of the Year in 2004. (Courtesy of Bill Osborne.)

The final year of competition for the *Miss Budweiser* was 2004, and she went out in style, winning the Columbia Cup with a four-heat sweep. (Courtesy of Bill Osborne.)

Dave Villwock won five out of seven races in 2004 and earned Budweiser their eighth consecutive national championship. However, with Budweiser's withdrawal from the sport, Villwock's future was uncertain. (Courtesy of Bill Osborne.)

Vintage boat collector David Bartush entered unlimited racing in 2005 by buying Kim Gregory's 15-year-old backup boat. This boat had won the Gold Cup three previous times—in 1988 as the *Circus Circus*, in 1991 as the *Winston Eagle*, and in 1994 as the *Smokin' Joe's*. Terry Troxell was hired to drive and gave Bartush a surprising Gold Cup win in his first-ever race. (Courtesy of Bill Osborne.)

Dave Bartush (left) and Terry Troxell celebrate their 2005 Gold Cup victory in Detroit. (Courtesy of Bill Osborne.)

J. W. Meyers started out the 2005 season driving for Ellstrom, but after a spectacular blow over in Detroit, he was replaced with Dave Villwock. Villwock drove the U-16 to a dominating win in the 2005 Columbia Cup. (Courtesy of Bill Osborne.)

When Dave Villwock took over the cockpit of the bright orange U-16, many fans were reminded of the way that Villwock and the bright red *Miss Budweiser* dominated the sport for many years. A standard joke in hydro circles that season was "orange is the new red!" (Courtesy of Bill Osborne.)

Billy Schumacher won the Gold Cup two times as the driver of the *Miss Bardahl* in 1967 and 1968. He returned to racing as an owner in 2006, when he purchased Bill Wurster's U-8 race team. Schumacher changed the boat's number to U-37 but kept Canadian Jean Theoret as driver. Theoret won the 2006 Gold Cup, making Schumacher one of only a handful of men to win the Gold Cup both as an owner and as a driver. (Courtesy of Bill Osborne.)

In 2006, Ted Porter of Decatur, Indiana, bought two of the former *Miss Budweisers* and renamed them *Formulaboats.com* and *Formulaboats.com II*. The new team kept the familiar red and white paint scheme of the *Miss Budweiser*. The rookie driver of *Formulaboats.com II*, Mike Allen, won only one race in 2006 but earned enough points to give Ted Porter a national championship in his first year as an owner. This photograph shows, from left to right, *Formulaboats.com* racing alongside the *Miss Elam Plus* and Ed Cooper's U-3 running for the start at the 2006 Columbia Cup. (Courtesy of Bill Osborne.)

In 2006, the wind was blowing hard all weekend. Racing was delayed for a while, but the weather was still an issue when racing resumed. Dave Villwock and the *Miss Elam Plus* caught a gust of wind and went airborne. (Courtesy of Bill Osborne.)

The boat reached an incredible height and began to tumble end over end. (Courtesy of Bill Osborne.)

The boat did almost two full revolutions in the air! (Courtesy of Bill Osborne.)

Almost as impressive as the *Elam*'s blow over accident is the hardworking crews' performance in getting the boat repaired and back out on the river in time to win the final heat. (Courtesy of Bill Osborne.)

The *Elam's* accident was not the only spectacular accident of the 2006 Columbia Cup. In this photograph, J. Michael Kelly in the U-13 blows over backwards. (Courtesy of Steve Conner.)

The right sponson of the U-13 barely misses the cockpit of the *Oh Boy! Oberto*, smashing into the horizontal stabilizer instead. (Courtesy of Steve Conner.)

The U-13 bounces on her sponson and pirouettes away. (Courtesy of Steve Conner.)

The U-13 continues to bounce out of the way of Steve David and the *Oh Boy! Oberto*. Neither driver was injured in this accident. (Courtesy of Steve Conner.)

Greg O'Farrell launched a new team in 2007. The U-48 *Miss Lakeridge Paving* was driven by rookie David Williams, this book's author. (Courtesy of Patrick Gleason.)

The *Miss Lakeridge Paving* was originally built in 1996 as *PICO American Dream*. This photograph shows Williams and the *Lakeridge* running to the start alongside Brian Perkins in the U-21 *Meyer's Auto Tech*. (Courtesy of Bill Osborne.)

Oh Boy! Oberto launched a brand new boat at the start of the 2007 season. Steve David drove the new silver, red, and green *Oberto* to second place in the Columbia Cup but finished the season with back-to-back wins in Seattle and San Diego. (Courtesy of Bill Osborne.)

David Bryant won Rookie of the Year honors driving Kim Gregory's U-10 *Hoss Mortgage Investors*. (Courtesy of Bill Osborne.)

Dave Villwock and the *Miss Elam Plus* were perfect in Tri-Cities in 2007. They set a qualifying record of 165.687 miles per hour and won all four of their heats to claim their third straight Columbia Cup. (Courtesy of Bill Osborne.)

As a hydroplane fan in the Northwest, Eric Ellstrom watched Bernie Little build a sporting dynasty, winning races, setting records, and claiming national championships. By the end of 2007, Eric and his *Miss Elam* had won the Columbia Cup five out of the last seven years. Many people feel that he is on his way to building the next great unlimited dynasty. (Courtesy of Bill Osborne.)

NATIONAL CHAMPIONS (1966–2007)

Year	Boat	Owner	Driver
1966	*Tahoe Miss*	Bill Harrah	Mira Slovak
1967	*Miss Bardahl*	Ole Bardahl	Bill Schumacher
1968	*Miss Bardahl*	Ole Bardahl	Bill Schumacher
1969	*Miss Budweiser*	B. Little-T. Friedkin	Bill Sterett
1970	*Miss Budweiser*	B. Little-T. Friedkin	Dean Chenoweth
1971	*Miss Budweiser*	B. Little-T. Friedkin	Dean Chenoweth
1972	*Atlas Van Lines*	Joe Schoenith	Bill Muncey
1973	*Pay N' Pak*	Dave Heerensperger	Mickey Remund
1974	*Pay N' Pak*	Dave Heerensperger	George Henley
1975	*Pay N' Pak*	Dave Heerensperger	George Henley
1976	*Atlas Van Lines*	Muncey Enterprises	Bill Muncey
1977	*Miss Budweiser*	Bernie Little	Mickey Remund
1978	*Atlas Van Lines*	Muncey Enterprises	Bill Muncey
1979	*Atlas Van Lines*	Muncey Enterprises	Bill Muncey
1980	*Miss Budweiser*	Bernie Little	Dean Chenoweth
1981	*Miss Budweiser*	Bernie Little	Dean Chenoweth
1982	*Atlas Van Lines*	Muncey Enterprises	Chip Hanauer
1983	*Atlas Van Lines*	Muncey Enterprises	Chip Hanauer
1984	*Miss Budweiser*	Bernie Little	Jim Kropfeld
1985	*Miller American*	Fran Muncey	Chip Hanauer
1986	*Miss Budweiser*	Bernie Little	Jim Kropfeld
1987	*Miss Budweiser*	Bernie Little	Jim Kropfeld
1988	*Miss Budweiser*	Bernie Little	Tom D'Eath
1989*	*Miss Budweiser*	Bernie Little	Tom D'Eath
1990	*Miss Circus Circus*	Bill Bennett	Chip Hanauer
1991*	*Miss Budweiser*	Bernie Little	Scott Pierce
1992	*Miss Budweiser*	Bernie Little	Chip Hanauer
1993	*Miss Budweiser*	Bernie Little	Chip Hanauer
1994*	*Miss Budweiser*	Bernie Little	C. Hanauer/M. Hanson
1995*	*Miss Budweiser*	Bernie Little	C. Hanauer/Mark Evans
1996	*PICO American Dream*	Fred Leland	Dave Villwock
1997*	*Miss Budweiser*	Bernie Little	D. Villwock/Mark Weber
1998	*Miss Budweiser*	Bernie Little	Dave Villwock
1999	*Miss Budweiser*	Bernie Little	Dave Villwock
2000	*Miss Budweiser*	Bernie Little	Dave Villwock
2001	*Miss Budweiser*	Bernie Little	Dave Villwock
2002	*Miss Budweiser*	Bernie Little	Dave Villwock
2003	*Miss Budweiser*	Joe Little	Dave Villwock
2004	*Miss Budweiser*	Joe Little	Dave Villwock
2005*	*Miss Elam Plus*	Ellstrom Family	J. W. Myers/D. Villwock
2006*	*Formulaboats.com II*	Ted Porter	Mike Allen
2007	*Miss Elam Plus*	Ellstrom Family	Dave Villwock

*There were a number of years when the National Champion driver was not the driver of the National Champion boat. In 1989 Chip Hanauer was the Driver's Champion, in 1991 Mark Tate won the Driver's Championship, and in 1994 and 1995 it was Mark Tate again. Tate won again in 1997. Steve David won in 2005 and 2006.

GOLD CUP WINNERS (1966–2007)

Year	Boat	Owner	Driver	Location
1966	*Tahoe Miss*	Bill Harrah	Mira Slovak	Detroit, MI
1967	*Miss Bardahl*	Ole Bardahl	Bill Schumacher	Seattle, WA
1968	*Miss Bardahl*	Ole Bardahl	Bill Schumacher	Detroit, MI
1969	*Miss Budweiser*	B. Little-T. Friedkin	Bill Sterett	San Diego, CA
1970	*Miss Budweiser*	B. Little-T. Friedkin	Dean Chenoweth	San Diego, CA
1971	*Miss Madison*	City Of Madison	Jim McCormick	Madison, IN
1972	*Atlas Van Lines*	Joe Schoenith	Bill Muncey	Detroit, MI
1973	*Miss Budweiser*	Bernie Little	Dean Chenoweth	Tri-Cities, WA
1974	*Pay N' Pak*	Dave Heerensperger	George Henley	Seattle, WA
1975	*Pay N' Pak*	Dave Heerensperger	George Henley	Tri-Cities, WA
1976	*Miss U.S.*	George Simon	Tom D'Eath	Detroit, MI
1977	*Atlas Van Lines*	Muncey Enterprises	Bill Muncey	Detroit, MI
1978	*Atlas Van Lines*	Muncey Enterprises	Bill Muncey	Owensboro, KY
1979	*Atlas Van Lines*	Muncey Enterprises	Bill Muncey	Madison, IN
1980	*Miss Budweiser*	Bernie Little	Dean Chenoweth	Madison, IN
1981	*Miss Budweiser*	Bernie Little	Dean Chenoweth	Seattle, WA
1982	*Atlas Van Lines*	Muncey Enterprises	Chip Hanauer	Detroit, MI
1983	*Atlas Van Lines*	Muncey Enterprises	Chip Hanauer	Evansville, IN
1984	*Atlas Van Lines*	Muncey Enterprises	Chip Hanauer	Tri-Cities, WA
1985	*Miller American*	Fran Muncey	Chip Hanauer	Seattle, WA
1986	*Miller American*	Fran Muncey	Chip Hanauer	Detroit, MI
1987	*Miller American*	Fran Muncey	Chip Hanauer	San Diego, CA
1988	*Miss Circus Circus*	Fran Muncey	J. Prevost/C. Hanauer	Evansville, IN
1989	*Miss Budweiser*	Bernie Little	Tom D'Eath	San Diego, CA
1990	*Miss Budweiser*	Bernie Little	Tom D'Eath	Detroit, MI
1991	*Winston Eagle*	Steve Woomer	Mark Tate	Detroit, MI
1992	*Miss Budweiser*	Bernie Little	Chip Hanauer	Detroit, MI
1993	*Miss Budweiser*	Bernie Little	Chip Hanauer	Detroit, MI
1994	*Smokin' Joe's*	Steve Woomer	Mark Tate	Detroit, MI
1995	*Miss Budweiser*	Bernie Little	Chip Hanauer	Detroit, MI
1996	*PICO American Dream*	Fred Leland	Dave Villwock	Detroit, MI
1997	*Miss Budweiser*	Bernie Little	Dave Villwock	Detroit, MI
1998	*Miss Budweiser*	Bernie Little	Dave Villwock	Detroit, MI
1999	*Miss Pico*	Fred Leland	Chip Hanauer	Detroit, MI
2000	*Miss Budweiser*	Bernie Little	Dave Villwock	Detroit, MI
2001	*Tubby's Grilled Submarines*	Mike Jones	Mike Hanson	Detroit, MI
2002	*Miss Budweiser*	Bernie Little	Dave Villwock	Detroit, MI
2003	*Miss Fox Hills Chrysler-Jeep*	Ed Cooper	Mitch Evans	Detroit, MI
2004	*Miss DYC*	Kim Gregory	Nate Brown	Detroit, MI
2005	*Miss Al Deeby Dodge*	Dave Bartush	Terry Troxell	Detroit, MI
2006	*Miss Beacon Plumbing*	Bill Schumacher	Jean Theoret	Detroit, MI
2007	*Miss Elam Plus*	Ellstrom family	DaveVillwock	Detroit, MI

APPENDIX

TRI-CITIES WINNERS (1966–2007)

Year	Race	Boat	Owner	Driver
1966	Atomic Cup	Miss Budweiser	Bernie Little	Bill Brow
1967	Atomic Cup	Miss Bardahl	Ole Bardahl	Bill Schumacher
1968	Atomic Cup	Miss Eagle Electric	Dave Heerensperger	Warner Gardner
1969	Atomic Cup	Myr's Special	Joe Schoenith	Dean Chenoweth
1970	Atomic Cup	Pay N' Pak's Lil' Buzzard	Dave Heerensperger	Tommy Fults
1971	Atomic Cup	Miss Madison	Miss Madison, Inc.	Jim McCormick
1972	Atomic Cup	Atlas Van Lines	Joe Schoenith	Bill Muncey
1973	APBA Gold Cup	Miss Budweiser	B. Little-T. Friedkin	Dean Chenoweth
1974	World Championship	Pay N' Pak	Dave Heerensperger	George Henley
1975	APBA Gold Cup	Pay N' Pak	Dave Heerensperger	George Henley
1976	Columbia Cup	Atlas Van Lines	Bill Muncey	Bill Muncey
1977	APBA Gold Cup	Atlas Van Lines	Bill Muncey	Bill Muncey
1978	Columbia Cup	Miss Budweiser	Bernie Little	Ron Snyder
1979	Columbia Cup	Atlas Van Lines	Bill Muncey	Bill Muncey
1980	Columbia Cup	Atlas Van Lines	Bill Muncey	Bill Muncey
1981	Columbia Cup	The Squire Shop	Bob Steil	Chip Hanauer
1982	Columbia Cup	The Squire Shop	Bob Steil	Tom D'Eath
1983	Columbia Cup	American Speedy Printing	Bob Taylor	Jack Schaefer Jr.
1984	APBA Gold Cup	Atlas Van Lines	F. Muncey-J. Lucero	Chip Hanauer
1985	Budweiser Columbia Cup	Miller American	F. Muncey-J. Lucero	Chip Hanauer
1986	Budweiser Columbia Cup	Miller American	Fran Muncey	Chip Hanauer
1987	Budweiser Columbia Cup	Miss Budweiser	Bernie Little	Jim Kropfeld
1988	Budweiser Columbia Cup	Miss Budweiser	Bernie Little	Tom D'Eath
1989	Budweiser Columbia Cup	Cooper's Express	Ed Cooper Sr. and Jr.	Mitch Evans
1990	Budweiser Columbia Cup	Miss Budweiser	Bernie Little	Tom D'Eath
1991	Budweiser Columbia Cup	Winston Eagle	Steve Woomer	Mark Tate
1992	Budweiser Columbia Cup	Miss Budweiser	Bernie Little	Chip Hanauer
1993	Budweiser Columbia Cup	Miss Budweiser	Bernie Little	Chip Hanauer
1994	Budweiser Columbia Cup	Miss Budweiser	Bernie Little	Chip Hanauer
1995	Budweiser Columbia Cup	Smokin' Joe's	Steve Woomer	Mark Tate
1996	Budweiser Columbia Cup	PICO American Dream	Fred Leland	Dave Villwock
1997	Budweiser Columbia Cup	PICO American Dream	Fred Leland	Mark Evans
1998	Budweiser Columbia Cup	Miss Budweiser	Bernie Little	Dave Villwock
1999	Budweiser Columbia Cup	Miss Budweiser	Bernie Little	Dave Villwock
2000	Budweiser Columbia Cup	Miss Elam Plus	Ellstrom family	Mark Evans
2001	Budweiser Columbia Cup	Znetix II	Fred Leland	Terry Troxell
2002	Budweiser Columbia Cup	Miss Elam Plus	Ellstrom family	Nate Brown
2003	Budweiser Columbia Cup	Llumar Window Film	Bill Wurster	Mark Evans
2004	Budweiser Columbia Cup	Miss Budweiser	Joe Little	Dave Villwock
2005	Budweiser Columbia Cup	Miss Elam Plus	Ellstrom family	Dave Villwock
2006	Tri-Cities Atomic Cup	Miss Elam Plus	Ellstrom family	Dave Villwock
2007	Lamb Weston Columbia Cup	Miss Elam Plus	Ellstrom family	Dave Villwock

Visit us at
arcadiapublishing.com

Printed in the USA
CPSIA information can be obtained
at www.ICGtesting.com
LVHW080156021024
792683LV00006B/24

9 781531 637460